Greater Than a Tour
Ebook and Audiobook f

C000140421

Greater Than a Tourist Book Series
Reviews from Readers

I think the series is wonderful and beneficial for tourists to get information before visiting the city.

-Seckin Zumbul, Izmir Turkey

I am a world traveler who has read many trip guides but this one really made a difference for me. I would call it a heartfelt creation of a local guide expert instead of just a guide.

-Susy, Isla Holbox, Mexico

New to the area like me, this is a must have!

-Joe, Bloomington, USA

This is a good series that gets down to it when looking for things to do at your destination without having to read a novel for just a few ideas.

-Rachel, Monterey, USA

Good information to have to plan my trip to this destination.

-Pennie Farrell, Mexico

Great ideas for a port day.

-Mary Martin USA

Aptly titled, you won't just be a tourist after reading this book. You'll be greater than a tourist!

-Alan Warner, Grand Rapids, USA

Even though I only have three days to spend in San Miguel in an upcoming visit, I will use the author's suggestions to guide some of my time there. An easy read - with chapters named to guide me in directions I want to go.

 -Robert Catapano, USA

Great insights from a local perspective! Useful information and a very good value!

 -Sarah, USA

This series provides an in-depth experience through the eyes of a local. Reading these series will help you to travel the city in with confidence and it'll make your journey a unique one.

-Andrew Teoh, Ipoh, Malaysia

GREATER THAN A TOURIST-IOWA USA

50 Travel Tips from a Local

Sharon Rubel

The statements in this book are of the authors and may not be the views of CZYK Publishing or Greater Than a Tourist.
First Edition
Cover designed by: Ivana Stamenkovic
Cover Image: https://pixabay.com/photos/dubuque-iowa-city-urban-buildings-1751444/

Image 1: https://commons.wikimedia.org/wiki/File:Desoto_Lake1.jpg I took this image on 6.24.2007 / Public domain
Image 2: https://commons.wikimedia.org/wiki/File:Amana_Colonies.JPG Kepper66 at en.wikipedia / Public domain
Image 3: https://commons.wikimedia.org/wiki/File:Des_Moines_skyline.jpg Tim Kiser (w:User:Malepheasant) / CC BY-SA (https://creativecommons.org/licenses/by-sa/2.5)
Image 4: https://commons.wikimedia.org/wiki/File:Survivor,_Northwest_Iowa_7-13_(22550505788).jpg Don Graham from Redlands, CA, USA - God bless it! / CC BY-SA (https://creativecommons.org/licenses/by-sa/2.0)

CZYK Publishing Since 2011.
Greater Than a Tourist

Lock Haven, PA
All rights reserved.
ISBN: 9798649361934

>TOURIST

50 TRAVEL TIPS FROM A LOCAL

BOOK DESCRIPTION

With travel tips and culture in our guidebooks written by a local, it is never too late to visit Iowa. Greater Than a Tourist-Iowa, USA by Author Sharon Rubel offers the inside scoop on The Hawkeye State. Most travel books tell you how to travel like a tourist. Although there is nothing wrong with that, as part of the 'Greater Than a Tourist' series, this book will give you candid travel tips from someone who has lived at your next travel destination. This guide book will not tell you exact addresses or store hours but instead gives you knowledge that you may not find in other smaller print travel books. Experience cultural, culinary delights, and attractions with the guidance of a Local. Slow down and get to know the people with this invaluable guide. By the time you finish this book, you will be eager and prepared to discover new activities at your next travel destination.

Inside this travel guide book you will find:

Visitor information from a Local
Tour ideas and inspiration
Save time with valuable guidebook information

Greater Than a Tourist- A Travel Guidebook with 50 Travel Tips from a Local. Slow down, stay in one place, and get to know the people and culture. By the time you finish this book, you will be eager and prepared to travel to your next destination.

OUR STORY

Traveling is a passion of the Greater than a Tourist book series creator. Lisa studied abroad in college, and for their honeymoon Lisa and her husband toured Europe. During her travels to Malta, an older man tried to give her some advice based on his own experience living on the island since he was a young boy. She was not sure if she should talk to the stranger but was interested in his advice. When traveling to some places she was wary to talk to locals because she was afraid that they weren't being genuine. Through her travels, Lisa learned how much locals had to share with tourists. Lisa created the Greater Than a Tourist book series to help connect people with locals. A topic that locals are very passionate about sharing.

TABLE OF CONTENTS

DEDICATION

This book is dedicated to my great-grandparents, both maternal and paternal, who came to the United States as immigrants and chose Iowa over all other states as the best place to call home. Their children loved this land and stayed to raise their own families here in the peaceful heart of the prairie.

ABOUT THE AUTHOR

Sharon Rubel is a writer, graphic designer, translator and ESL teacher living in Grinnell, Iowa. She was born in the capital city of Iowa, Des Moines, and though she's lived in other states, she always called Iowa home and never failed to come back to this beautiful state. Sharon loves to travel, and even though she's been to over a dozen countries and most of the US, the green fields and blue skies of Iowa will always be her home.

HOW TO USE THIS BOOK

The *Greater Than a Tourist* book series was written by someone who has lived in an area for over three months. The goal of this book is to help travelers either dream or experience different locations by providing opinions from a local. The author has made suggestions based on their own experiences. Please check before traveling to the area in case the suggested places are unavailable.

Travel Advisories: As a first step in planning any trip abroad, check the Travel Advisories for your intended destination.
https://travel.state.gov/content/travel/en/traveladvisories/traveladvisories.html

FROM THE PUBLISHER

Traveling can be one of the most important parts of a person's life. The anticipation and memories that you have are some of the best. As a publisher of the Greater Than a Tourist, as well as the popular *50 Things to Know* book series, we strive to help you learn about new places, spark your imagination, and inspire you. Wherever you are and whatever you do I wish you safe, fun, and inspiring travel.

Lisa Rusczyk Ed. D.
CZYK Publishing

WELCOME TO
> TOURIST

DeSoto lake at DeSoto National Wildlife Refuge

Street in the Amana Colonies, Iowa

Downtown Des Moines, Iowa as viewed from the south.
Photographed from the south bank of the Raccoon River.

Farm in rural Northwest Iowa

Des Moines Iowa Climate

	High	Low
January	30	13
February	35	17
March	49	29
April	62	41
May	73	52
June	82	62
July	86	67
August	84	64
September	77	55
October	64	43
November	48	30
December	35	18

GreaterThanaTourist.com

Temperatures are in Fahrenheit degrees.
Source: NOAA

In Iowa, we take care of people.
That's all I think I need to say.

Iowa Congressman Steve King

Iowa has something for absolutely everyone! As I sit here writing, I'm looking out the window at one of the most beautiful spring days I've ever seen – sunshine, blooming crabapple trees and flowers everywhere, and the sweet scent of lilacs fills the air. The farmers have this year's harvest in the ground, and the corn and soybeans they have planted are starting to sprout in the gentle spring rains.

If you love all four seasons, Iowa is the place for you! From fresh spring breezes to warm, sometimes downright hot summer sunshine, to fall harvests and crisp autumn nights, to winter with real snowball fights and cozy fires, Iowa has it all.

Besides an infinite variety of weather, Iowans come in all varieties, too. From summertime tractor parades and county fairs to international corporations and performances, you can see why Iowa is the best of all worlds. Come with me and explore my state and see why I will always call Iowa my home!

Iowa
United States

1. WHY DID YOU COME TO IOWA?

Here in Grinnell, where I live, we have a small 4-year college called…wait for it…Grinnell College. It has a worldwide academic reputation, attracting students from all 50 states and at least 26 countries. The college recruits local Grinnell families to be "host families" for international students who are far away from home. A few years ago, I signed up for the program.

My first student was a young Korean woman who had grown up in Shanghai, the largest city in China. I asked her why she wanted to come to little Grinnell to complete her university training, instead of at a major university in China or Korea. "I can be myself here," she told me. She went on to say that in Iowa, she felt like she was making a difference, like she had found a place where she was welcomed and appreciated for who she was. She had found a place to belong.

That's Iowa!

2. IOWA, ONE WHO PUTS TO SLEEP?

Iowa has been a place to belong since 1846, on land originally purchased from the French as part of the Louisiana Purchase in 1803. There are lots of theories about how Iowa got its name. The Dakota tribe had a word, "ayuxbe," meaning "sleepy ones," or "one who puts to sleep." Some think it was used jokingly by the Dakota to describe the Baxoje tribe from Iowa (the tribe we now know as the Iowa.) The word was pronounced "Aiouez" by the French, and by the English as "Ioway."

But sleepy? Maybe to an outsider, but from the big city to rural towns, Iowa is far from sleepy as we'll soon see.

3. WHAT'S THE BEST TIME OF YEAR TO TRAVEL TO IOWA?

The answer is: Any time! You will find amazing things to do and see in absolutely any season of the year. Of course, summertime will be the busiest season, with farmer's markets, outdoor activities and festivals. Summertime sees each big city and small town hosting a summer festival, from Hot Dog Days in Clarion to the Des Moines Arts Festival, an award-winning event featuring artists from across the United States. The absolute do-not-miss event of the summer is the Iowa State Fair, showcasing the best of Iowa's county fairs.

In the spring, Iowans celebrate the arrival of warm weather, and can be found firing up the grills, venturing out to the golf courses, and welcoming the return of many farmer's markets around the state. As you drive the rural highways, you'll see farmers planting, livestock wandering the rolling hills, and gorgeous sunrises and sunsets as the days get longer. Don't forget Tulip Time in Pella, a beautiful spring celebration of the Dutch heritage. You'll experience parades, Dutch delicacies, and thousands of multi-colored tulips blooming everywhere.

Fall has to be my favorite Iowa season. Fall in Iowa is everything you will see in a children's story – raking leaves, harvesting apples at Iowa's many orchards, picking pumpkins at the pumpkin farms, and so much more. Take a drive along the Mississippi

River and be charmed by the gorgeous fall foliage. Sample the best of Iowa's wineries and breweries and enjoy Oktoberfest in the Amana Colonies.

Winter in Iowa can be chilly, with temperatures in the teens and twenties, but there can also be days with high temperatures into the fifties. But snow and cold don't keep Iowans inside very often. You'll find ice fishing, snowmobiling and skiing, both cross country and downhill. Don't miss cheering for the Iowa Wild, Iowa's professional hockey team, with family-friendly games October through April. Take a sleigh ride at Jester Park, go snowshoeing at the Ledges State Park, or cut your own Christmas tree at one of Iowa's many Christmas Tree farms.

No matter when your journey brings you to Iowa, you'll find so many things to see and do that you'll be planning your next trip back before you even arrive home.

4. GETTING AROUND IN IOWA

Iowa is crisscrossed by lots of well-maintained highways. If you don't plan to bring your own car or rent a car, you might find your options for traveling the state somewhat limited. I-80 runs east and west through the middle of the state. Driving from Council Bluffs, you can reach Davenport in around 5 hours. I-35 divides Iowa in half from north to south, Missouri to Minnesota.

You can fly into Des Moines International Airport (DSM) on many national carriers. On a smaller scale, the Eastern Iowa Airport (CID) in Cedar Rapids, has flights on Delta, Allegiant, American, United and Frontier. You can fly on American to and from Chicago at the Waterloo Regional Airport (ALO).

Amtrak has two Iowa routes, however neither one services Des Moines. Jefferson and Greyhound bus lines also service Iowa. Check their websites for details.

In the larger cities, you will find public bus transportation, and limited taxi service. Parking is rarely a problem, unless you are visiting a large venue like a concert or sporting event, but even then, there will be places to park within walking distance of your goal.

You'll almost always have cell phone service from your car, especially along all the major highways and interstates and in populated areas. Keep an eye on your signal, however, if you're out in the more rural areas between towns.

5. SOME APPS TO HELP YOU

Iowa 511

Iowa 511 is maintained by the Iowa Department of Transportation, and can provide information on all interstates, U.S. highways and state highways. It can update you on winter road conditions, construction, and accidents.

KCCI 8 News

This app from the CBS television affiliate in Des Moines can provide you with up-to-date news and weather information, including interactive radar to keep an eye on approaching weather systems.

Iowa Travel Guide by Triposo

This extensive app helps you plan your trip to Iowa with features that help you discover book lodgings, find good places to eat and be entertained, and personalize your trip. It provides maps that you can use offline. You can also use the maps to help you create and share city walks.

6. AREN'T THERE TORNADOES IN IOWA?

Iowa, as well as most of the Midwest, has a reputation for severe weather. Iowa averages fewer than 50 tornadoes in a season, but wait! Remember that Iowa is a rural state, so many of these storms pass over farmland. While they can and do cause significant damage to rural towns and farms, they rarely last very long, and there is almost always enough warning for people to be able to take shelter. You can always monitor the weather systems if the weather looks threatening, and forecasters will be ever-present to tell you where the storm systems are heading and how likely they would be to produce severe weather.

If you need to be on the road during your stay in Iowa, try not to travel if there is severe weather on the way. Sign up for text alerts from The Weather Channel or the KCCI 8 news app. Television monitors at rest areas along interstate highways will provide weather information. If you are traveling in a mobile home or RV, be sure to always take stock of where you are, the weather forecast, and have a plan of where you will take shelter, just in case.

All that said, I have lived in Iowa all my life, and though I've had to shelter in the basement a couple of times, I have never seen or experienced a tornado. They do happen, and though property damage can be substantial, fatalities are rare in a normal season. If you travel safe and travel smart, you shouldn't have to worry overly much about severe weather in Iowa.

The same advice goes for winter blizzards and springtime flooding. Not super common, but they do happen, so just be aware and monitor the situation carefully. You'll have lots of advice from local weather forecasters online, on TV, and on the radio as you're traveling.

7. ARE THERE WILD ANIMALS IN IOWA?

Iowa is very safe, ranking as the sixth safest state! That said, there are a few things to be wary of if you like to be outdoors.

Don't worry about meeting wildlife more dangerous than a deer. The main danger you will face from a deer is hitting one of them with your car as they jump out in front of you on almost any highway, from country roads to interstates. Be especially cautious during the late fall and early spring. They are very active at dusk, which is unfortunately the time of day when you may be least able to spot them waiting to pounce on the side of the road.

Other "critters" that might want to play chicken with your car include opossums and raccoons in the country, and in the cities, squirrels and rabbits.

More "exotic" wildlife has been spotted in Iowa on occasion, including mountain lions, black bears and wolves. Most of these are wanderers and don't stay long, with the occasional moose taking a summer hike down from Minnesota before heading back home because he's getting too hot.

Iowa's insect population is more dangerous than its prairie wildlife. If you're outdoors in the summer, watch out for mosquitos and ticks. We do have black widow and brown recluse spiders, but these are rare. I've never seen one, and they don't like bright and busy places where visitors enjoy being. We have four species of dangerous snakes, including timber rattlesnakes that live mostly in the south and east of the state, again in undisturbed habitats. In my entire life, I think I've only seen three snakes in the wild... harmless garden variety snakes that were hurrying from one hiding place to another.

Check out the website of the Iowa Department of Natural Resources for more information on Iowa wildlife and current statistics on their populations.

8. OUI, WE ARE FROM IOWA

We've already discovered that our state's name came from an Indian word by way of the French.

Famous explorers Father Jacques Marquette and Louis Joliet were the first known Europeans to come through the area in 1673. You could say they came the easy way – instead of crossing the Appalachian Mountains, these French explorers came from Canada by way of Lake Michigan, to the Wisconsin River and from there to the Mississippi.

By the middle of the 18th century, France controlled more area in what is now the continental United States than any other European country. The area from the Mississippi to the Rocky Mountains became New France, later known as the Louisiana Purchase, when President Thomas Jefferson bought it from Napoleon in 1803.

Iowa retains much of its French history, with place names like Lafayette, Montpelier, Le Claire, and Dubuque (named after explorer Julien Dubuque), just to name a few. The name of our capital city, Des Moines, comes from the French "Rivière des Moines," or "River of the Monks," that flows through the middle of the city.

Even the state flag of Iowa was modeled after the flag of France. Divided into three bands, one blue, one white, and one red, it has the state name on the white middle band, along with an eagle carrying the state motto, "Our liberties we prize and our rights we will maintain."

9. IOWA'S EARLY INHABITANTS

Because of this settlement by the French and other Europeans, Iowa's ethnicity tends to be more Northern European – English, German, and Scandinavian. Another reason for this is that these ethnic groups were drawn here by similarities in climate to their home countries.

The Sac and Fox Tribe of the Mississippi is the only federally recognized native American tribe still in Iowa. Their tribal name is Meskwaki, or "Red Earth People." As native Americans were pushed out of their lands by the governments, Iowa allowed the Meskwaki to buy land. Over the next 150 years, they expanded their settlement near Tama.

10. MESKWAKI POW WOW

If your trip brings you to Iowa in August, don't miss the annual Meskwaki Pow Wow. You are more than welcome to come and enjoy this fabulous cultural event! Today, it is more of a social gathering where you can experience the ancient dances and songs, as well as more contemporary offerings. The Meskwaki perform dances that have been handed down for generations in full traditional dress, and they welcome all visitors to join them for this three-day event.

11. "IS THIS HEAVEN? NO, IT'S IOWA"

Remember the 1989 movie Field of Dreams, with Kevin Costner? In 2017, the film was selected for preservation in the United States National Film Registry for being "culturally, historically, or aesthetically significant."

The movie was filmed on two farms near Dyersville in northeastern Iowa near Dubuque, and an empty warehouse in Dubuque was used to shoot many of the interior scenes. The last scene, with the long string of cars and headlights driving into the farm, became a community event. The nearby town of Dyersville was blacked out, and local extras drove their vehicles to the field.

You can still visit the Field of Dreams Movie Site, where you can tour the baseball field and visit the farm. Schedule a tour of the home, too, where you'll learn about the original Lansing family and the home's rebirth as the Kinsella family homestead.

12. THE BRIDGES OF MADISON COUNTY

Speaking of movies shot in Iowa, don't forget 1969's Cold Turkey, starring Dick Van Dyke, and featuring Randy Newman's first film soundtrack. The final climactic scenes from the movie Twister, with Helen Hunt and Bill Paxton, were shot in several locations near Ames and Eldora.

Most of the filming for Sylvester Stallone's 1978 movie F.I.S.T. was done in Dubuque, chosen because the older sections of the town looked more like Cleveland of the 1930s than the actual city of Cleveland.

But perhaps the most famous movie filmed in Iowa is The Bridges of Madison County, starring Clint Eastwood and Meryl Streep. Streep was also nominated for the Best Actress award for her role as Francesca Johnson. It was filmed on location in rural Madison County, and the towns of Winterset and Adel.

After the movie was released, the home was available for tours, but it was badly damaged by a suspicious fire in 2003, along with one of the covered bridges.

You can still take a guided Bridges of Madison County Tour through downtown Winterset. Drive the Covered Bridges Scenic Byway and explore the history of these beautiful and unique structures. The Madison County Covered Bridge Festival is held every year on the second full weekend in October, with food, antiques, crafts, entertainment, artisan demonstrations, and best of all, guided bus tours of these important landmarks of Iowa's history.

13. "TALK LOW, TALK SLOW AND DON'T SAY TOO MUCH"

While you're in Winterset following in Clint Eastwood's footsteps, don't miss Winterset's even bigger claim to fame – the birthplace of Marion Mitchell Morrison, better known as John Wayne.

More than a million visitors have toured this historic restored home to view the largest collection of John Wayne memorabilia in existence, from original movie posters and scripts to contracts, artwork and even one of his latest customized cars. Relax in theater seats from Grauman's Chinese Theater and watch a documentary celebrating his life and film legacy.

In late May, to celebrate the Duke's birthday, you can attend a fabulous two-day John Wayne Birthday Celebration, featuring special guests and great entertainment. Check out their website for current tour information and tickets.

14. THE DAY THE MUSIC DIED

If you go north on Interstate 35 to the town of Clear Lake, you can visit the Surf Ballroom. For many, this is a cultural icon as well as the place where some say rock and roll changed forever, with the deaths of Buddy Holly and the other members of the Winter Dance Party tour.

The Surf Ballroom was one of the first ballrooms in the state to feature rock 'n' roll, and the big-name acts featured there made it a "must play" stop for Holly, Ritchie Valens, The Big Bopper, and Dion. You can still attend Winter Dance Parties at the Surf in late January and February, a three-day celebration of the lives and legacies of these rock 'n' roll legends that were gone from us too soon.

The plane crash site is six miles from Clear Lake in a lonely stretch of farm country. The spot on the road is marked by a big pair of black glasses, and it's a long walk to the crash site, but you can see that lots of people have made the trek by the path worn into the soil. At the site, you'll see that it's pretty DIY, but it's obvious that fans still visit today and remember the day the music died.

15. "RIGHT HERE IN RIVER CITY"

While we are talking about great music, you'll want to be sure to take a trip to Mason City to see the birthplace and museum of musician Meredith Willson, composer of The Music Man. Visit Music Man Square, a 1912 streetscape with shops all recreated to match the set of the 1962 movie starring Robert Preston and Shirley Jones.

You'll find an interactive museum showcasing Meredith Willson memorabilia and music-related exhibits. Take a self-guided or guided tour any weekday afternoon, and don't forget to visit the Meredith Willson house, just a few steps away. This restored 1895 Queen Anne house was his birthplace and boyhood home. Even if you aren't a music fan, you can see what life was like in the early 19th century for an upper middle-class family in Iowa.

Meredith Willson is honored at the North Iowa Band Festival each year in Mason City. Enjoy the largest free marching band competition in the Midwest, along with free musical entertainment, family friendly activities, and more. If you're near Mason City on Memorial Day weekend, be sure to check it out.

16. AMERICA'S FAVORITE MUSICAL PATRIOT

No musical tour of Iowa would be complete without a trip to Clarinda to see the birthplace of Glenn Miller, "America's Favorite Musical Patriot" and quintessential big band leader of the forties and fifties.

If you're in Iowa in June, grab tickets to the Glenn Miller Festival, featuring world-famous big band orchestras, brass bands, and a free concert on the Clarinda town square with dinner, dancing and a swing dance competition to follow. The festival is a feast of a weekend that you won't want to miss!

While you're here for the festival, be sure to visit the Glenn Miller Birthplace Museum and visitor center, which tells the story of Glenn's rise to stardom and his service in World War II with artifacts and special exhibits. Nearby, you can tour the restored

1904 home where he was born, showcasing more Glenn Miller memorabilia and photos from The Glenn Miller Story, starring James Stewart and June Allyson.

17. "MOST LEGENDS HAVE THEIR BASIS IN FACTS"

The last Iowa celebrity we're going to visit actually hasn't been born yet. James T. Kirk, captain of the Starship Enterprise, will be born in Riverside, Iowa on March 22, 2228. This is a fact.

In 1985, Riverside mayor Steve Miller, a die-hard Trekkie, was reading Gene Roddenberry's 1968 book, Making of Star Trek, and noticed that Kirk would be born in a small town in Iowa. Miller decided to claim the glory for Riverside, changing its summer festival from River Fest to Trek Fest. A barber shop he owned became Kirk's birthplace, and the town slogan became "Where the Trek Begins."

All his hard work paid off, because Riverside was identified as Kirk's hometown in the 2009 movie Star

Trek, starring Chris Pine as the intrepid and unruly Captain Kirk. Riverside has also been featured in at least two Star Trek novels.

The Voyage Home Riverside History Center sells copies of Roddenberry's statement declaring the truth of this future history. Travel to Riverside for Trek Fest at the end of June and celebrate the future birth of our hero with a parade, 5K run, fireworks, and more. This is Iowa small town living at its best.

18. EAT YOUR WAY THROUGH IOWA

No Iowa festival would be complete without food. Now that we've visited some of our most famous celebrity sites and festivals (even though we didn't make it to Ashton Kutcher's birthplace in Cedar Rapids), let's take a look some of Iowa's culinary favorites that you should definitely try.

When people think of Iowa, and Midwestern food, most people think of meat and potatoes. And most people would be right. Iowa is the number one pork producing state in the nation. At any one time there are approximately 22 million hogs being raised in

Iowa – compare that to our population of a little over 3 million people. Iowa contributes 25 percent of the nation's pork supply.

Pork can be the star of any meal - breakfast (sausage and bacon), lunch (pulled pork sandwiches with Cookies BBQ sauce, or burgers with bacon) and dinner (grilled Iowa Chops with potatoes in any form.) Wrap your Iowa Chops with bacon and magic will happen on your taste buds.

We love our breaded pork tenderloins - big frisbee-sized platters of deep-fried deliciousness served on a normal-sized bun with pickles and mustard. Each summer, Iowans vote on the best tenderloin in the state. If you look on the Iowa Pork Producers website, you'll see lots of past winners so you can create your own personal best pork tenderloin contest, including my personal favorite, Darrell's Place, in tiny Hamlin.

While you're happily munching away on your super sandwich (fries with that, please) take a look at the Tenderloin Trail, also on the Iowa Pork Producers website, that will lead you to twelve of the best tenderloins in Iowa. Download the "Conquer the

Tenderloin Trail" passport, collect all twelve stamps, and earn yourself a free t-shirt.

19. A SANDWICH THAT IS MAID RITE

While we are talking about meat and potatoes, no culinary tour of Iowa is complete without trying a classic Maid Rite – that delicious and uncontrollable loose meat sandwich on a bun. Not your classic sloppy joe with tomato sauce, the Maid Rite is loose ground beef braised and flavored with a variety of different liquids, from pickle juice to Worcestershire sauce to a touch of BBQ sauce. Everyone makes homemade Maid Rites differently, but to go to a Maid Rite restaurant and order one is just a little piece of heaven.

Maid Rite sandwiches were created in 1926 in Muscatine, by a butcher named Fred Angell. Maid Rite is now a franchise with 32 restaurants in Iowa and surrounding states. It was the very first restaurant chain to offer a drive through service. It also earned a spot on the Travel Channel's "Bizarre Foods" series. But don't worry! Taste this delicious Iowa institution

- but if you'd rather have a tenderloin or a pulled pork sandwich, you can get one of those at a Maid Rite restaurant, too. With fries.

20. NADA ES IMPOSIBLE

In 1961, Richard and Antonia Mosqueda opened a "little hole in the wall" restaurant in Des Moines, calling it Tasty Tacos. Today they have six family owned and operated restaurants in the Des Moines area, serving their own famous deep-fried "fluffy" flour tacos, created by Antonia, and other delicious homemade food. Antonia, the aunt of my friend Betty's husband, still oversees this family-run Des Moines institution. And that's Iowa – we are all connected to each other, and we support and care in as many ways as we can.

Food Network featured Tasty Tacos in its "50 States 50 Tacos" series, and guess which taco won in Iowa? My brother lives in San Antonio, Texas, Mexican food capital of the world, and he still comes home to Iowa and heads straight to Tasty Tacos. Grab yourself another t-shirt, hot sauce or seasoning mix to take home while you're there!

21. TAKE YOUR DINNER TO THE RAILS

For a little more adventurous dining experience, don't miss the Sunset BBQ Dinner Train, in Boone. This is dining on the rails as it was in the golden age of train travel in the US.

The trip lasts for two hours, taking you through the beautiful Des Moines River Valley and over the 156' tall Bass Creek High Bridge for a fantastic view of the beauty of rural Iowa. At this writing, the BBQ menu includes… da da da…your choice of pulled pork, sliced brisket, or smoked chicken, and potatoes, this time in the form of creamy potato salad.

The Sunset BBQ dinner train only runs on Saturday evenings in March and April, but the Boone and Scenic Valley Railroad offers other lunch and dinner trains that you can choose from. Visit their website for more information.

22. ONE OF ALTON BROWN'S FAVORITE RESTAURANTS

Imagine a Chinese restaurant in the heart of downtown Des Moines, closing after nearly a hundred years in business. Enter the new owners of Fong's Pizza, who decided they couldn't let such a landmark restaurant pass into obscurity. Keeping all the original décor of the King Ying Low restaurant, they morphed the menu into an amazing fusion of Asian and Italian. To top it all off, they added a tiki/dive bar.

Fong's Pizza was voted Best Pizza in Iowa by Food Network magazine and has received lots of other kudos and awards. After only ten years in business, they've opened three other Iowa locations. You have to try the Crab Rangoon Pizza. There's nothing else quite like it! And get yourself a t-shirt, while you're at it.

23. GET INSPIRED WITH IOWA WINES AND BEERS

Iowa has over 100 wineries and another 100 breweries, with many more on the way. No visit to

Iowa is complete without enjoying a glass of these world class beverages.

One of the best ways for visitors to check out the Iowa wine and beer scene is to follow a wine or beer trail, highlighting the best Iowa has to offer. There are many to choose from, so unfortunately I can only highlight a few. Do some research of your own and don't miss the chance to check out some of Iowa's most beautiful landscapes as you travel the state in search of your next new favorite wine or beer.

Amana Colonies Wine Trail
Because of their German heritage, the Amana Colonies boast Iowa's oldest micro-brewery and have several award-winning wineries. Find a list of places to have a sip at the Amana Colonies website.

Iowa Wine Trail
Travel the upper Mississippi Valley wine region and sample well-crafted wines and ciders such as Brick Arch Winery in West Branch, Eagles Landing Winery in Marquette, Tabor Home Winery in Baldwin, and more superb family-owned wineries. Wineries can be visited almost daily. Consider

staying the night at one of their bed-and-breakfast partners.

I80 Wine Trail

From east to west along Interstate 80, you'll find fantastic wineries within 10 miles of the highway. Take a ten-minute detour off your cross-country drive and experience the ambiance of local wineries like Breezy Hills Winery in Minden, Fireside Winery (my personal favorite) in Marengo, and the Buchanan House Winery in Tipton. Pick up a few bottles to share with your friends and be sure to check for t-shirts!

The Iowa Wine Growers website contains a complete list of Iowa's wine trails.

For beer aficionados, you'll find a list of all seven Iowa beer trails plus an interactive map at the Iowa Beer website. Drive the Northeast Iowa Beer Trail from Dubuque to Bellevue, or do the Des Moines Metro Beer Trail, with 15 stops in the metro area.

You can also download the Iowa Wine and Beer App. Search for wineries and breweries near you and see what's currently on tap. You'll also find lists of events and special offers.

24. A TRUCKER'S DISNEYLAND

As you're traveling I-80, be sure to stop in Walcott, west of Davenport, and see another of Iowa's impressive claims to worldwide fame, the Biggest Truck Stop in the World. Established in 1964, it's grown and expanded until now it could be called a small city, with both fast food and sit-down restaurants, a complete automotive supply store, and trucker services like a barbershop, a chiropractor, a dentist, and more.

In July, you can attend the Truckers Jamboree, a three-day celebration of truckers and the trucking industry. See the Super Truck Beauty Contest, two fireworks displays, and eat great food at the Iowa pork chop cookout. Don't miss the Trucker Olympics or the evening concerts with great country bands.

Also visit the Iowa 80 Trucking Museum, a dream of I-80 Truck Stop founder Bill Moon. See his collection of rare trucks and watch short films about the history of trucking in America.

25. IOWA'S BEST SUMMERTIME OFFERING

There are so many other deserving family-owned and operated restaurants and food producers in Iowa to mention, and I wish there was room here to highlight them all. Before your trip, please google "Hometown restaurants in Iowa" to find the best of Iowa's eateries.

For now, though, no discussion of Iowa food would be complete without mentioning Iowa's summertime staple, the farmers' market. Usually open from April through October, these outdoor venues feature the best of Iowa produce. If you can imagine it, you can probably find it at one of Iowa's farmers' markets.

Des Moines' Downtown Farmers' Market is certainly one of the largest with over 300 vendors. Here you can also find stands and food trucks that will serve you breakfast and lunch, as well as fresh, home grown ingredients and local crafts. You can find farmers' markets in nearly every county and many cities and towns throughout the state.

If you're driving down a peaceful rural highway, you might also see local farmers selling their goods at a roadside stand. July is the best time for this, and you'll see fresh garden tomatoes, zucchini, sweet corn, and perhaps cucumbers, melons, and green beans, to name just a few.

In June, you can pick your own strawberries at one of Iowa's many strawberry farms, such as family owned Hinegardner's Orchard, near Montour. Later in the summer, you can pick melons, plums, squash and pumpkins there, and be sure to join them for apple picking and Cider Day in the fall. Before you go, check their website for exact information as far as dates and availability, because as they say, Mother Nature has a huge say in what's available in any given year.

26. RECREATING IOWA'S FARMING HISTORY

Of course, farming is central to Iowa life. According to data from Iowa State University, fully a third of Iowa's population is rural. In Poweshiek county, where I live, over half of our county's residents live outside of any city limits. The only counties where the urban population outnumbers the rural population are the counties that host our largest cities.

You can celebrate the history of Iowa farm families at Living History Farms in Urbandale, a Des Moines suburb, where you'll experience an interactive outdoor museum of rural life in the Midwest. The "living history" involves creating real simulations of rural and small-town life through the centuries.

You can visit a 1700's Ioway farm, an 1850's pioneer farm, the re-created historic 1876 town of Walnut Hill, and a 1900's horse-powered farm – all hosted by historic interpreters who are actually farming and working the site. You can interact with these guides and they are happy to answer any questions you might have.

Bring the kids for this fantastic glimpse into Iowa's history. Find more information on the Living History Farms website.

27. HISTORICAL ROOTS

All of Iowa's original residents brought their own farming methods, their culture, and their wisdom to make Iowa the multi-cultural state it is today. Iowa abounds with tributes to these early settlers and you can see their heritage preserved in many museums across the state.

The National Czech and Slovak Museum and Library in Cedar Rapids is a Smithsonian affiliate. Early Czech immigrants to Iowa settled in farming communities, and later immigrants began to settle in Cedar Rapids in the 1850s. By 1900, there was a thriving Czech- speaking community in Cedar Rapids, and today more people of Czech ancestry live in Cedar Rapids than in any other city in the world, except for Prague. In May, visit Houby Days, a weekend event that celebrates Czech heritage in Cedar Rapids with a parade and other fun family activities.

The Museum of Danish America, in Elk Horn, celebrates and preserves the heritage of Danes in Iowa with a beautiful museum and park, and a hiking trail that includes Danish-designed fitness equipment.

Nearby, you can visit an authentic Danish windmill, and have authentic Scandinavian food at The Danish Table restaurant.

Memorial Day weekend in Elk Horn features Tivoli Fest, an annual celebration of Danish heritage including windmill tours, folk dancing, and the Annual World Aebleskiver Eating Championship. I've been here many times, as my own heritage is Danish, and I have to confess that the Museum of Danish America is my favorite heritage museum. You haven't lived until you've had roast duck for Christmas dinner, which my Danish grandmother made every year.

Visit the German American Heritage Center in Davenport, showcasing the history of German immigrants to the Midwest. Located in the old Standard Hotel on the Davenport riverfront, it's a classic example of high Victorian commercial architecture. The 1900 U.S. Census documented that over half the citizens of Iowa and five other states in the upper Midwest were German immigrants or their descendants.

Vesterheim Norwegian American Museum, in Decorah, features twelve historic buildings with artifacts and history of Norwegian settlement in Iowa, including a Folk Art School and library. Celebrate Nordic Fest in Decorah each July, a celebration of Scandinavian heritage, culture and of course, food. More than 1.5 million visitors from around the world have attended this fun festival since its inception in 1967.

The African American Museum of Iowa opened in 1994 and has become the leading educational resource on African American history in Iowa. It offers permanent and traveling exhibits, educating people about the history of African Americans in Iowa with summer camps and workshops.

Visit the Swedish American Museum in Swedesburg for a look at Swedish immigrant life and memorabilia and see Iowa's largest Dala horse.

The Meskwaki maintain the Meskwaki Cultural Center and Museum in Tama to give visitors a glimpse into the tribe's rich cultural legacy.

I'm sure I've missed many other great historical museums, so apologies in advance! Besides these ethnic heritage museums, most Iowa counties have a county historical museum. Here you'll get a glimpse into Iowa pioneer life, unique to that particular county. Be sure to google your Iowa interest, and you'll find lots of opportunities to explore. Don't forget the State Historical Museum of Iowa, in Des Moines' East Village, for a treasure trove of information about Iowa history and culture, and for a listing of other historical sites in Iowa.

28. THE EIGHTH WONDER OF THE WORLD

Let's look at some other fabulous historical sites in Iowa for just a moment. Again, I wish I could list them all, but let's just touch on some of the most famous.

In the small town of West Bend, you'll find the Grotto of the Redemption. The Iowan magazine has called the Grotto "a miracle in stone." It consists of nine separate grottos, each focusing on a scene in the life of Christ. This is the largest man-made grotto in the world and contains the largest collection of precious stones and gems found anywhere in one location.

The Grotto of the Redemption was created by German immigrant Father Paul Matthias Dobberstein. As a young seminarian, Father Dobberstein became critically ill with pneumonia, and promised that if the Blessed Virgin Mary would intercede and heal him, he would build a shrine in her honor. He came to West Bend in 1898, and for ten years he stockpiled rocks and precious stones, beginning the work on the Grotto in 1912.

You can read more about the history of the Grotto on its website, westbendgrotto.org. The shrine is open 24/7, and there is no admission fee (though donations are accepted). You can also attend mass at nearby Saints Peter and Paul Church. There is camping with hookups available. Don't miss this amazing site.

29. "IF YOU DREAM IT, YOU CAN BUILD IT"

During a 1921 visit to Salisbury, England, Des Moines based cosmetics magnate Carl Weeks and his wife Edith visited The Kings House, a 15th century manor. This became the inspiration for their Des Moines home, now called The Salisbury House.

This historic Tudor and Jacobethan Revival home contains 42 rooms and was built and furnished for a final cost of three million dollars, in 1920s currency. You'll see authentic 16th century English oak woodwork, flintwork and rafters, transported from England, that date back to the time of Shakespeare. You can also see the Weeks family's collection of original art, tapestries, and unique furnishings.

Salisbury House is now open to the public, with self-guided and guided tour options from Wednesday through Sunday. It hosts a variety of public events and programs throughout the year, including a proper English afternoon tea, called Tea at the Castle. You can also see William Shakespeare's plays come to life during the summer months on the majestic south terrace and gardens.

Like murder mysteries? The Murder Mystery Dinner is hosted at the Salisbury House at various times during the year.

30. TIPTOE THROUGH THE TULIPS

The beautiful city of Pella is home to Dutch immigrants who settled here in 1847. Pella has long preserved its history and welcomes visitors year-round to the Historical Village, Vermeer Windmill, and the Scholte House. For a breathtaking weekend in early May, you can visit the city festival called Tulip Time.

Many of the events at Tulip Time are free. Choose from three afternoon parades, three lighted evening parades, and grandstand events including Dutch dancers. Food is a huge part of Tulip Time! You can find local restaurants and local organizations alike serving authentic Dutch meals prepared for the festival. Don't leave, I repeat, do not leave Tulip

Time without a trip to the local bakeries on the town square, where you'll find traditional Dutch treats including Dutch letters. Brave the long lines, it's worth it.

While you are in Pella, you can also visit the boyhood home of Wyatt Earp. Its 18th century Dutch style is normally only seen in the Netherlands or in the eastern United States. Take a tour of the Vermeer Windmill, the tallest working windmill in North America. It was built in the Netherlands, disassembled and shipped to Iowa, and re-assembled in Pella in 2002.

Be sure to check the websites of these family-friendly attractions for current opening hours and dates.

31. AMANA COLONIES

Some of Germany's immigrants to Iowa settled in the Iowa River Valley in east-central Iowa in 1855, forming seven villages now known as the Amana Colonies. Sometimes mistaken for Amish, these German Pietists also kept themselves separate and maintained a communal and self-sufficient lifestyle.

Today the Amana Colonies are known for their restaurants and craft shops. Stop at the Amana Heritage museum to learn more about the Pietists and their Iowa history. Amana restaurants typically serve food family style, meaning that large servings of dishes are set on the table and are passed around, rather like a big Thanksgiving meal.

You can find small craft and gift shops, with handmade products as well as imported items. Take a class at the Amana Art Guild, or buy local art from the galleries. Do you like hiking and biking? The Iowa River Valley near the Amana Colonies has lots of nature trails for you to explore.

Amanians love their festivals! Depending on the time of year you visit Iowa, try Winterfest in January or Maifest in early May. During Maifest, you'll enjoy ethnic music and dance, and also the World on Wheels Food Truck Fare, bringing world cuisines to the Amana Colonies. Grab a punchcard for the Wine, Beer and Chocolate Walk, sample the offerings, and claim your Maifest glass.

Wurst Festival in August celebrates the German tradition of sausage making…and what goes great with wurst? Beer, of course. Music, food, and games abound, as well as the Dachshund Derby, a fun competition for our little sausage-shaped friends.

What German community worth its salt could exist without Oktoberfest? Amana holds its celebration in early October. Oktoberfest at the Amana Colonies is one of the longest running festivals in Iowa and features more special events and competitions, food, and music with a German flair.

Tannenbaum Forest is a Christmas celebration held every weekend in the month between Thanksgiving and Christmas. It brings Christmas back to a much simpler time, as local businesses and organizations decorate trees and fill a century-old dairy barn with the sights and sounds of Christmas.

You'll find information about the Colonies, their history and culture, and all kinds of festivals and special events on their website.

32. A COMMITMENT TO BALANCE AND NATURAL LAW

Four miles north of Fairfield, in southeastern Iowa, you will find the planned community of Maharishi Vedic City. The city plan and buildings are based on Maharishi Sthapatya Veda, said to be a system of architecture and design from ancient India. This concept was conceived by the Maharishi and a vision for a Vedic town was begun in 1991. The town of a little over a thousand residents sits on land purchased from local farmers and converted into native prairie, wetland and forest, as well as an area for the town itself.

The city operates an organic farm that supplies fruits and vegetables to restaurants from Iowa City to Chicago. Each citizen visits the two Golden Domes in the center of town, the largest such domes in the country, twice a day to practice Transcendental Meditation.

In Fairfield itself is the Maharishi University of Management, and you can book a private tour of the city and the university any day of the week with advance notice. Tours of the campus include the Golden Dome, the Argiro Center, the Vedic Observatory, and the Sustainable Living Center.

33. FORM OUT OF FUNCTION

Famous architect Frank Lloyd Wright leaves eleven of his masterpieces in Iowa, and two of them are open for tours.

The Stockman House in Mason City is open year-round for group and private tours. The nearby Robert E. McCoy Architectural Interpretive Center houses exhibition space and a gift shop promoting local artisans.

Cedar Rock, a home Wright designed and build for Lowell and Agnes Walter, is located in Cedar Rock

State Park near Quasqueton, a small town in north central Iowa. One of Wright's most complete designs, almost everything in the home bears his touch. Cedar Rock was donated to the Iowa Department of Natural Resources by Lowell Wright on his death in 1981. Tours are available from May through October for the cost of a donation to the Friends of Cedar Rock organization.

Louis Sullivan, Wright's mentor, also has a presence in Iowa. Here in Grinnell, where I live, is Merchants National Bank, one of Sullivan's eight Jewel Box banks. This cubical building, representing the stability and security needed by a bank, has elaborate stonework and terracotta ornamentation on the exterior with beautiful stained glass windows, hence the name Jewel Box. The Merchants National Bank is open year-round on weekdays from 8-5, and currently houses the Grinnell Chamber of Commerce. There are two other Jewel Box banks in Iowa, one in Cedar Rapids and one in Algona.

34. SUMMER OF THE ARTS

Besides being Iowa's original capital city, Iowa City is the home of the University of Iowa, the internationally recognized Writer's Workshop, and the Summer of the Arts. The Summer of the arts includes three festivals: the Iowa Arts Festival, the Iowa City Jazz Festival, and the Soul & Blues Festival.

The Iowa Arts Festival happens in early June, and features over 100 local and national visual artists. There are also creative and educational activities for kids, food vendors serving regional and ethnic dishes, and musical performances. The Iowa Arts Festival is a weekend-long celebration of the visual arts.

The Iowa City Jazz Festival is a three-day July weekend of live jazz performances by well-known national and international jazz musicians as well as rising talent. You'll also find great food and enjoy fireworks on Saturday evening.

The Soul & Blues Festival, in late July, celebrates the Black experience through the local and global reach of Soul & Blues music. Enjoy food, dancing, music, and art of African and African American communities.

Summertime in Iowa gives visitors and residents alike tons of opportunities for even more musical celebrations. Try America's River Festival in Dubuque each June, Steamboat Days on the riverfront in Burlington, and the Cedar Rapids Freedom Festival, June and July in Cedar Rapids, to name just a few.

35. A WEEKEND OF RODEO FUN

Iowa cities and towns celebrate their farming and ranching heritage with lots of rodeo events across the state. Here are just a couple of highlights:

Tri-State Rodeo
The nation's top cowboys descend on Fort Madison each September to show off their prowess at this premier rodeo event. This rodeo is ranked as one of the top five large outdoor rodeos in the nation and attracts thousands of visitors. Big name performers

perform each Friday and Saturday night at this PRCA and WPRA sanctioned rodeo.

Cherokee Rodeo

From Thursday to Saturday in late May you'll love this family-friendly event with a Kid's Rodeo and free kids' activities, including a petting zoo, a parade, and pony rides. Adults will find Western vendors, a beer garden, quality rodeo entertainment and a live concert after the rodeo at the event center in downtown Cherokee.

Iowa's County Fairs and Rodeos

In the summer months leading up to the Iowa State Fair in August, Iowa counties have their own county fairs. Some feature rodeo competitions and you can get up close and personal with the event at these smaller festivals – but not too close!

Iowa's county fairs are a personal and intimate celebration of Iowa farm families and their traditions. Try the Jones County Fair in Monticello, or the If you're in Iowa in the summertime, definitely find the closest county fair to your location and the time of your visit. You won't be sorry!

36. AMERICAN GOTHIC

Tucked away in tiny Eldon, in southeastern Iowa, you'll find the Carpenter Gothic style house that was used by artist Grant Wood in his famous 1930 painting, American Gothic. Tour hours for the house are limited, so be sure to check the website for current information. The adjacent Visitor Center is open daily, and you can see historical exhibits as well as choose a costume and prop for your own photo op in front of this cultural icon. Admission to the house and visitor center is free, and donations are gratefully accepted.

You can learn more about Grant Wood by taking a trek to Cedar Rapids and visiting the Grant Wood Studio, where he lived and worked from 1924 to 1935. This is the studio where American Gothic was painted. The Armstrong Visitor Center promotes educational programs and artistic activities. Currently it's open on weekends from April through December for tours, with no admission charge.

Grant Wood left his mark on Iowa, and you can travel the Grant Wood Trail that stretches 75 miles from Anamosa to the Mississippi.

37. SPEAKING OF THE MISSISSIPPI...

Be sure to spend some time in this picturesque area of our lovely state. Driving the Iowa Great River Road will take you to storybook towns and beautiful landscapes all along Iowa's eastern border. Let's start in the north and see some of the highlights.

Effigy Mounds National Monument
The Effigy Mounds are prehistoric native American burial and ceremonial mounds, dating from as far back as 500 B.C. Learn more in the visitor center, open year-round, seven days a week.

Backbone State Park
Backbone State Park is Iowa's first state park. If you love the outdoors, there is something for you at Backbone. You'll find 2000 acres of recreation for fishers, campers, and every other kind of outdoor enthusiast. Check out the Backbone Bluegrass Festival in late July each year.

Dubuque

Named for French explorer Julien Dubuque
(remember him?), Dubuque is a beautiful city situated
on bluffs overlooking the Mississippi. Ride the
Fenelon Place Elevator, the world's shortest and
steepest railway, from the business district on the
riverfront up to the residential areas on top of the
bluffs. Learn about the natural history of the
Mississippi River region at the National Mississippi
River Museum and Aquarium. Take a dinner or
sightseeing cruise on the American Lady yacht, or
just walk the streets of this unique Iowa city.

American Pickers and Antique Archaeology

Antique Archaeology, in Le Claire, is the home
base for the American Pickers show on the History
Channel. Check out this two-story former fabrication
shop that houses some of the best picks and a new
merchandise store.

Eulenspiegel Puppet Theater

The Eulenspiegel Puppet Theater at Owl Glass
Puppetry Center in West Liberty presents
performances and workshops and hosts the annual
West Liberty Children's Festival. It tours nationally

and internationally and is open year-round by appointment only.

Mississippi Valley Fair

The Mississippi Valley Fair is a five-day concert extravaganza in Davenport each year in early August, with nationally known entertainers and shows. The fairgrounds also offer other events year-round, including concerts, dirt track racing, and Bingo games on Sunday - Bingo being an Iowa community staple.

Steamboat Days

Steamboat Days is an outdoor music festival on the Mississippi riverfront in Burlington. Country music fans will be in heaven, but fans of rock 'n' roll and throwback bands will find lots to love as well.

George M. Verity Riverboat Museum

Take a trip back to a time when steamboats ruled the Mississippi at the George M. Verity Riverboat Museum in Keokuk. And when you're in Keokuk, be sure to pronounce it the way the natives do – not KEE-uh-kuck, but KYOH-kuck.

I'm sure I've missed dozens of super attractions, events, and experiences along the 550-mile Iowa portion of the Great River Road. If you check it out yourself, I know you'll find more places that you will love to explore further.

38. GEOGRAPHY UNIQUE IN THE WORLD

Just as the Mississippi River creates Iowa's eastern border, the Missouri River forms Iowa's western border. The Loess Hills are bluffs on the Iowa side of the Missouri that were formed when the glaciers retreated and the fine silt, or Loess soil, from the riverbed was blown into huge dune fields. Over time, these dunes eroded into the sharp bluffs we see today. The Loess Hills of Iowa are the deepest deposits of loess soil in the world. The only comparable deposits are located in Shaanxi, China in the Yellow River Valley.

Just like the Mississippi's Great River Road, you can drive the Loess Hills Scenic Byway. It runs for 220 miles along Iowa's western border. The Lewis and Clark Trail, the Oregon Trail, the Mormon Trail and the California Trail all traverse this byway.

Several rare plants and animals call the Loess Hills home.

Visitors can enjoy many nature areas along the way. The Loess Hills State Forest, the Dorothy Pecaut Nature Center, and the Hitchcock Nature area, among others, are all dedicated to preserving this piece of Iowa's natural history. Visit the Lewis and Clark Monument in Council Bluffs, the site of their historic meeting with Otoe and Missouri tribal leaders. Get a breathtaking view of the Missouri River from the scenic overlook there.

The Loess Hills Scenic Byway is beautiful any time of year, but schedule your trip for early to mid-October for the best show of autumn color around. If you love the idea of driving in autumn to see the leaves, check out the Weekly Color Report on the Travel Iowa website.

39. AMERICA'S MAIN STREET

In 1912, Indianapolis businessman Carl Graham Fisher proposed a highway that would span the continent from coast to coast. He named it the "Lincoln Highway," believing that it would appeal to patriotic Americans. The route was carefully chosen without regard to including large cities or scenic areas, hoping only to provide a quick and direct route from Times Square in New York to Lincoln Park in San Francisco.

Many Iowans believed that inclusion or exclusion from this route would make or break their town. They schemed in as many ways as possible to get the route to include them. Affectionately known as "The Main Street Across America," it more or less parallels its newer neighbor, Interstate 80, from the Mississippi to the Missouri rivers. Some towns and cities still have main streets named after the Lincoln Highway, such as Lincoln Way in Ames.

In places, the route is not drivable anymore, but if you fancy a gentle trip through Iowa's sometimes colorful roadside attractions and points of local interest, such as Brucemore Mansion in Cedar Rapids, the historic Squirrel Jail in Council Bluffs (the only three-story revolving jail in the world), or RVP~1875 in Jefferson, the world's leading historical heirloom furniture shop and museum, give it a try.

You could literally spend weeks travelling Iowa's Lincoln Highway and Historical Scenic Byway, seeing all the unique experiences Iowa has to offer.

40. IOWA'S MOST UNIQUE STATE PARK

Step back in geological time with a visit to Maquoketa, along the Mississippi River, and Maquoketa Caves State Park. This collection of 16 limestone caves is linked by six miles of beautiful trails with rock formations and overlooks that provide a great hiking experience. Some caves are accessible by walking, such as Dancehall Cave, and others can only be explored by crawling. Bring your flashlight and old clothes for a trip you won't soon forget. Your kids will love it!

Artifacts such as pottery and stone tools have been found in the caves and surrounding areas, so we know that the area has been occupied for hundreds or even thousands of years. Learn more about the geology of caves and the earliest inhabitants of the park at the interpretive center and take a video tour of the park if you're unable to manage the rugged terrain. Open on weekends during the summer.

The caves stay around 52 degrees Fahrenheit year-round, so bring warm clothes, even in summertime. Maquoketa Caves State Park is part of the Iowa Parks System, and as such it offers camping, picnic shelters, and more.

41. TAKE TIME TO DREAM

The Big Treehouse and Gardens is the personal hobby and project of Mick Jurgensen and his family in Marshalltown. Begun in 1983, it's a 12-level, 55-foot high treehouse in Shady Oaks Campground, complete with electricity, running water, and much more. Push button activated voice recordings, recorded by Mick's grandmother, offer more information. Benches and porch swings give you places to pause during your climb for great views of treetops, gardens, and walkways.

Steps to the first 11 levels make the ascent easy. Level 12 is reached by ladder, and the 60-step Spiral Staircase, added in 2002, takes you up or down from level 11. Hammered dulcimer music adds nostalgia to this natural setting.

Visits to The Big Treehouse are by appointment only, and guided tours are provided by Mick's mother and grandmother during fair weather days and warm months only. Visit the website for more information.

42. THE IOWA GREAT LAKES

In northwest Iowa, a beautiful chain of seven glacier-carved lakes extends from the Minnesota border and includes Iowa's largest natural lake, Spirit Lake. Spring-fed West Lake Okoboji is the centerpiece, and this area is definitely a year-round playground for vacationers.

Besides great camping, swimming, and other outdoor activities, visitors come to Okoboji in early August for the Okoboji Blue Water Festival, a free musical celebration to raise public awareness of water quality issues. This event has attracted some big-name performers and thousands of concert goers.

In July, come to Spirit Lake for BRASL, the Bike Ride Around Spirit Lake. Sign up for a 15, 25, or 50-mile bike ride. Pre-register for the race and get a free t-shirt to add to your by now quite substantial Iowa t-shirt collection.

Visit the Iowa Great Lakes Maritime Museum, see a show at the Okoboji Summer Theater, or take the family to Ranch Okoboji, with over 3 acres of fun including mini-golf and the Tyotees Wild Mining Adventure.

In 1889, Wesley Arnold build a 60-foot wooden toboggan-style waterslide on the south shore of West Lake Okoboji. This was the first attraction at what would become Arnold's Park Amusement Park. Today, Arnold's Park is a premier concert venue and theme park for family friendly fun. Cruise the Queen II, a large steamer as famous as the park itself, that will take you on an aquatic tour of West Lake Okoboji and can be chartered for private events.

43. WHAT IN THE WORLD IS RAGBRAI?

You can take part in BRASL, the annual bike ride around Spirit Lake, or if you're feeling energetic and adventurous, try RAGBRAI – the Register's Annual Great Bike Ride Across Iowa. Bikers come from all over the world to take part in this week-long event created in 1973 when two writers at the Des Moines Register newspaper challenged each other to ride across Iowa on a bicycle, then write about it. An estimated 300 Iowans joined them for the first ride.

Today, RAGBRAI is the oldest, longest, and largest bike touring event in the world. In 2019, it attracted over 20,000 riders from all over the globe. Local Iowa communities chosen as overnight stops for the current year's route go all out, offering riders accommodations, sustenance, and entertainment along the way.

RAGBRAI isn't for the faint of heart. If you want to participate, remember that this takes place in July, which can be one of the hottest times of the year in Iowa, with temperatures that can reach into the 90s and humidity levels to match. Bring lots of sunscreen! Drink lots of water, be sure to register, and make sure you get the t-shirt!

44. THE IOWA SKIES ARE ALIVE

After the RAGBRAI bikers dip their bike wheels in the Mississippi, signaling the end of the ride, the next step for central Iowans is to look up into the sky to see the brilliant colors and cheerful shapes of over a hundred hot air balloons. Late July and August sees the arrival of competitors for the National Balloon Classic, where skilled pilots compete each morning and evening, when the winds are the most stable, for nine days.

Bring your family to the Memorial Balloon Field in Indianola to watch the balloons and enjoy skydiving and musical entertainment. Book a balloon ride in advance and create a lifelong memory. Nighttime skies come alive during Dawn Patrols and Nite Glow flights. During a Nite Glow flight, pilots blast the propane burners, releasing a burst of fire into the balloon and making them glow like a sea of Chinese lanterns. A truly magical sight.

45. NOTHING COMPARES

After RAGBRAI and the National Balloon Classic, more than a million people from around the world gather for the Iowa State Fair. It attracts performers, competitors, and vendors from across the country. The Iowa State Fair hosts the largest food department of any state fair, and one of the world's largest livestock shows.

It began in 1854 and has been held in Des Moines on the State Fairgrounds since 1886. The fair begins on the second Thursday of August and lasts for 11 days. This is a really good idea, because there's so much to see that it's difficult to do in one day! You'll be able to watch draft horse competitions, dog shows, and see performers from wood carvers to jewelry makers. Visit the livestock pavilions and see if you can even count the variety of animals raised on Iowa's farms.

Try classic State Fair food – corn dogs, funnel cakes, and fresh lemonade. Taste deep-fried delicacies like Oreo cookies and Snicker bars, not to mention deep-fried butter. In 2015, you could buy 70 different versions of food-on-a-stick, including pork chops on-a-stick. Walk through the children's garden and see the blue-ribbon winners from Iowa's 99 county fairs. You may see presidential candidates stumping if it's an election year. Check out the contests, including rooster crowing, outhouse racing, and pigeon rolling.

Probably the one of the most well-known attractions at the Iowa State Fair is the Butter Cow. The Butter Cow first made her appearance at the 1911 State Fair. These days, you can see not only the butter cow, but other creative butter sculptures like a butter rendition of DaVinci's Last Supper, kept cool in the refrigerated display cases of the Agriculture Building.

Headline artists perform each night on the Grandstand stage, and you can watch sprint car races at the Iowa State Fair Speedway.

You can also camp at the fairgrounds, which is the best way to see and experience it all. Truly, as the slogan says, nothing compares to the Iowa State Fair.

46. THE FASTEST SHORT TRACK ON THE PLANET

After watching the sprint car races at the fairgrounds, NASCAR fans will not want to miss the Iowa Speedway in Newton, known as the Fastest Short Track on the Planet because of the unparalleled speeds IndyCar drivers reach when racing at the Iowa Speedway. IndyCar practice laps on this 7/8 mile oval track have reached 186 mph, 10 mph faster than recorded at any other short track.

Iowa Speedway was designed with input from NASCAR Hall of Famer Rusty Wallace and completed in 2006.

Visitors can camp on the Speedway grounds in a regular campground or in a unique, terraced campground overlooking the track that can host up to 40,000 spectators. Book a driving experience or a ride along experience with the Rusty Wallace Racing Experience, the largest racing school in the United States.

I've been to the Iowa Speedway, and I have to say that though I'm not a huge racing fan, I really enjoyed my visit. The Speedway is a modern, clean, and spacious venue and the fans are totally dedicated to the sport and very Iowa hospitable and courteous. When you go, just be sure to bring your noise-cancelling headphones, especially if your seats are on the lowest tier, close to the track. Most folks will be wearing them. The Iowa Speedway is a great day trip if your base is Des Moines, as it's only 30 miles east of the capital city. Check the Iowa Speedway website for dates and times for its varied events, including the IndyCar Series, NASCAR Nationwide Series, and the NASCAR Truck Series.

Also, try sprint car racing at the Knoxville Raceway dirt track, where the Knoxville Nationals are hosted. While you're in Knoxville, visit the National Sprint Car Hall of Fame and Museum, the only museum in the world dedicated to the history of sprint car racing. Open seven days a week, 362 days a year.

47. PROFESSIONAL SPORTS IN IOWA

Car racing isn't the only pro sport Iowa offers its fans! If you're in Des Moines, you won't want to miss being in the stands for any of these great teams.

Iowa Cubs

Get to Des Moines' Principal Park and catch a home run ball hit by the Iowa Cubs, AAA affiliate of the Chicago Cubs.

The Iowa Barnstormers and the Cedar Rapids Titans

IFL arena football at its best, with games from April through June in Des Moines and Cedar Rapids.

Des Moines Roosters

The Des Moines Roosters are Iowa's only Australian Football club, formed in March of 2009. Australian football is a rough and tumble blend of football and soccer, like ice hockey in the summer with no padding! The Roosters compete against other midwestern teams and are building the Australian football culture here in Iowa.

Des Moines Buccaneers and the Iowa Wild

Speaking of ice hockey, it's alive and well in Iowa! The USHL has five teams in Iowa – the Cedar Rapids RoughRiders, the Sioux City Musketeers, the Des Moines Buccaneers, the Dubuque Fighting Saints, and the Waterloo Black Hawks.

The AHL Iowa Wild, an affiliate of the Minnesota Wild, play at Wells Fargo Arena in downtown Des Moines. Check the schedule and buy tickets online, and don't forget to get the t-shirt!

Iowa Wolves

The Iowa Wolves are an NBA G league team, an affiliate of the Minnesota Timberwolves. They're Iowa's official minor league basketball team, and they play at Wells Fargo Arena in Des Moines.

Des Moines Menace

This USL league two soccer team plays at Drake Stadium in Des Moines.

The John Deere Classic

This PGA tour golf event is hosted each year in the Quad Cities, played annually in the week before the

British Open. What, you may well ask, are the Quad Cities? Ask any Iowan and they will tell you that the Quad Cities straddle the Mississippi River in southeastern Iowa, and include Davenport and Bettendorf, Iowa, and Moline (incuding East Moline) and Rock Island, Illinois. The Quad Cities area is unique among Mississippi River communities, because the river flows from east to west as it passes through.

48. NCAA EXCELLENCE

No discussion of sports in Iowa would be complete without mentioning Iowa's four NCAA Division I schools. The University of Iowa Hawkeyes, in Iowa City, are perhaps the most well-known nationally, and their football team has had post-season appearances consistently since 1981's Rose Bowl appearance.

The Iowa State University Cyclones also play Division I sports, though are a little lesser known than the Hawkeyes. In Iowa, the rivalry is fierce between the two schools and their alumni. The annual September football game between the Cyclones and the Hawkeyes is a tailgating, keg-tapping event that people from all over the state will happily give you their opinion about even if you don't ask.

The Cyclones and the Hawkeyes also have historically famous wrestling programs, with the Hawkeyes coached at one point by Olympic and World gold medal winner, Iowan Dan Gable, who wrestled for Iowa State during his student years.

Iowa's other two Division I schools are the University of Northern Iowa, in Cedar Falls, and Drake University, a private 4-year college in Des Moines.

49. PRINCIPAL RIVERWALK

Near the Iowa Cubs stadium in Principal Park, the Des Moines River bisects the city and also the downtown area. The Principal Riverwalk is a 1.2-mile pedestrian walkway with bridges that connect both sides of the city. Take a peaceful Saturday afternoon walk along the river, after a busy morning at the Court Avenue Farmers' Market.

Along the Riverwalk, you'll find the Robert D. Ray Asian Gardens, honoring this former Iowa Governor's compassionate leadership and his provision for Asian refugees to Iowa.

Also along the Riverwalk, you'll find the Simon Estes Ampitheater, dedicated to this Iowa native's international opera career. Take a break in the West River Front Park, Rotary Riverwalk Park, or Muto Recreation Area, then continue along the walk to see contemporary commissioned art pieces that highlight important events in the history of Des Moines.

Close to the Riverwalk in Des Moines' East Village, you can explore the Greater Des Moines Botanical Garden, seven acres of indoor and outdoor gardens, and enjoy a break in the Trellis Café.

If you love to garden, consider a visit to the Better Homes and Gardens Test Garden, located in downtown Des Moines at the headquarters of Meredith Corporation, Grand Avenue and 15th Street. The Test Garden is a testing ground for plants, a display garden, and a photography studio for the company's publications and websites. Visiting times are limited to Fridays from noon to 2:00 pm, May through October, since it is also a working garden. Garden staff is available to answer questions, and group tours can be scheduled.

50. HAUNTED IOWA

Iowa has its own cache of supernatural happenings and spooky sightings. Here are just a few highlights. You can visit all these places, hear the stories, and check it out for yourself!

The Historic Hotel Julien

This elegant and fully restored hotel in Dubuque dates back to 1839 and has hosted guests such as Abraham Lincoln and Mark Twain. However, guests and locals insist it's one of the most haunted buildings in Iowa.

Guests and staff have reported seeing a male dressed in vintage clothing floating through the upper floors. Many people think this is Al Capone, who used this hotel as a hideout during Prohibition.

The Klondike Hotel

The Klondike Hotel in Manilla is a popular spot for paranormal investigators, and a number of interesting EVP recordings have been captured here. Over the years, many guests have chosen to leave their accommodation here because of paranormal activity in their rooms, such as rocking chairs that move by themselves.

The Blackhawk Hotel

In 1986, after falling ill at a nearby club, Cary Grant died in his room at the Blackhawk Hotel in Davenport. Over the years, there have been reported sightings of the deceased actor in the hallways. A meth lab exploded in the hotel in 2006, and other ghosts are said to inhabit the building, including a woman in either a red or blue evening gown. The beautifully restored Blackhawk Hotel is also a popular spot for paranormal investigations.

Edinburgh Manor

Edinburgh Manor in Scotch Grove was used as a poor farm, mental institution and retirement home for decades. At least 80 inmates died on the farm and many of them are said to still roam the halls and grounds. If you are brave, you can take an evening and nighttime tour of Edinburgh Manor through American Hauntings Tours.

Villisca Axe Murder House

An entire family and their two guests were murdered by an intruder in this small home in Villisca, now said to be haunted by the ghosts of those who perished. You can take a daytime or overnight tour of the house, check their website for more information.

There are so many more. Try the Redstone Inn and Suites in Dubuque, the Ashton Cemetery in Mingo, or the Mason House Inn in Bentonsport. Find more information on Hauntedrooms.com, where they also advise you that the best way to experience these paranormal events is to book a room for the night, so you can spend a significant amount of time at the location.

I know I've missed so many of the famous and not-so-famous experiences and events that make my home state one of the best places in the country to live, work, and raise a family. You'll want to do your own research to discover for yourself what you want to see on your visit to this jewel of the prairie. Iowa.

TOP REASONS TO BOOK THIS TRIP

Seasons: Iowa is beautiful. It has four unique seasons, and we have events and activities that allow you to enjoy them all to their fullest potential.

Food: You will never go hungry in Iowa, with access to farm-fresh produce, meats, wines and beers that can easily compete with any flashy five-star restaurant.

Friendly and welcoming people: You can be sure, when you're walking down Main Street or driving through Iowa's small towns, that folks will be friendly and welcoming, and will probably even wave at you as you drive by.

OTHER RESOURCES:

Traveliowa.com – for anything and everything about traveling in Iowa

Iowadnr.gov – the official website for Iowa's Department of Natural Resources

www.511ia.org – gives up to the minute road conditions and traveling information

https://iowadot.gov/iowa_transportation_map/ - online version of the current Iowa road map

kcci.com – CBS affiliate offering accurate weather information and radar

PACKING AND PLANNING TIPS

A Week before Leaving

- Arrange for someone to take care of pets and water plants.

- Email and Print important Documents.

- Get Visa and vaccines if needed.

- Check for travel warnings.

- Stop mail and newspaper.

- Notify Credit Card companies where you are going.

- Passports and photo identification is up to date.

- Pay bills.

- Copy important items and download travel Apps.

- Start collecting small bills for tips.

- Have post office hold mail while you are away.

- Check weather for the week.

- Car inspected, oil is changed, and tires have the correct pressure.

- Check airline luggage restrictions.

- Download Apps needed for your trip.

Right Before Leaving

- Contact bank and credit cards to tell them your location.

- Clean out refrigerator.

- Empty garbage cans.

- Lock windows.

- Make sure you have the proper identification with you.

- Bring cash for tips.

- Remember travel documents.

- Lock door behind you.

- Remember wallet.

- Unplug items in house and pack chargers.

- Change your thermostat settings.

- Charge electronics, and prepare camera memory cards.

READ OTHER
GREATER THAN A TOURIST
BOOKS

Greater Than a Tourist- Geneva Switzerland: 50 Travel Tips from a Local by Amalia Kartika

Greater Than a Tourist- St. Croix US Birgin Islands USA: 50 Travel Tips from a Local by Tracy Birdsall

Greater Than a Tourist- San Juan Puerto Rico: 50 Travel Tips from a Local by Melissa Tait

Greater Than a Tourist – Lake George Area New York USA: 50 Travel Tips from a Local by Janine Hirschklau

Greater Than a Tourist – Monterey California United States: 50 Travel Tips from a Local by Katie Begley

Greater Than a Tourist – Chanai Crete Greece: 50 Travel Tips from a Local by Dimitra Papagrigoraki

Greater Than a Tourist – The Garden Route Western Cape Province South Africa: 50 Travel Tips from a Local by Li-Anne McGregor van Aardt

Greater Than a Tourist – Sevilla Andalusia Spain: 50 Travel Tips from a Local by Gabi Gazon

Children's Book: *Charlie the Cavalier Travels the World* by Lisa Rusczyk Ed. D.

> TOURIST

Follow us on Instagram for beautiful travel images:
http://Instagram.com/GreaterThanATourist

Follow *Greater Than a Tourist* on Amazon.

>Tourist Podcast

>T Website

>T Youtube

>T Facebook

>T Goodreads

>T Amazon

>T Mailing List

>T Pinterest

>T Instagram

>T Twitter

>T SoundCloud

>T LinkedIn

>T Map

> TOURIST

At *Greater Than a Tourist*, we love to share travel tips with you. How did we do? What guidance do you have for how we can give you better advice for your next trip? Please send your feedback to GreaterThanaTourist@gmail.com as we continue to improve the series. We appreciate your constructive feedback. Thank you.

METRIC CONVERSIONS

TEMPERATURE

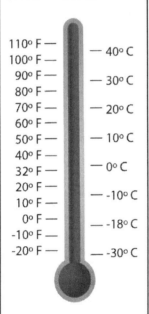

110° F — — 40° C
100° F —
90° F — — 30° C
80° F —
70° F — — 20° C
60° F —
50° F — — 10° C
40° F —
32° F — — 0° C
20° F —
10° F — — -10° C
0° F —
-10° F — — -18° C
-20° F — — -30° C

To convert F to C:

Subtract 32, and then multiply by 5/9 or .5555.

To Convert C to F:

Multiply by 1.8 and then add 32.

32F = 0C

LIQUID VOLUME

To Convert:.................Multiply by
U.S. Gallons to Liters................ 3.8
U.S. Liters to Gallons 26
Imperial Gallons to U.S. Gallons 1.2
Imperial Gallons to Liters....... 4.55
Liters to Imperial Gallons 22
1 Liter = .26 U.S. Gallon
1 U.S. Gallon = 3.8 Liters

DISTANCE

To convert ....Multiply by
Inches to Centimeters 2.54
Centimeters to Inches 39
Feet to Meters........................ .3
Meters to Feet 3.28
Yards to Meters 91
Meters to Yards 1.09
Miles to Kilometers 1.61
Kilometers to Miles............ .62
1 Mile = 1.6 km
1 km = .62 Miles

WEIGHT

1 Ounce = .28 Grams
1 Pound = .4555 Kilograms
1 Gram = .04 Ounce
1 Kilogram = 2.2 Pounds

TRAVEL QUESTIONS

- Do you bring presents home to family or friends after a vacation?

- Do you get motion sick?

- Do you have a favorite billboard?

- Do you know what to do if there is a flat tire?

- Do you like a sun roof open?

- Do you like to eat in the car?

- Do you like to wear sun glasses in the car?

- Do you like toppings on your ice cream?

- Do you use public bathrooms?

- Did you bring a cell phone and does it have power?

- Do you have a form of identification with you?

- Have you ever been pulled over by a cop?

- Have you ever given money to a stranger on a road trip?

- Have you ever taken a road trip with animals?

- Have you ever gone on a vacation alone?

- Have you ever run out of gas?

- If you could move to any place in the world, where would it be?

- If you could travel anywhere in the world, where would you travel?

- If you could travel in any vehicle, which one would it be?

- If you had three things to wish for from a magic genie, what would they be?

- If you have a driver's license, how many times did it take you to pass the test?

- What are you the most afraid of on vacation?

- What do you want to get away from the most when you are on vacation?

- What foods smell bad to you?

- What item do you bring on ever trip with you away from home?

- What makes you sleepy?

- What song would you love to hear on the radio when you're cruising on the highway?

- What travel job would you want the least?

- What will you miss most while you are away from home?

- What is something you always wanted to try?

- What is the best road side attraction that you ever saw?

- What is the farthest distance you ever biked?

- What is the farthest distance you ever walked?

- What is the weirdest thing you needed to buy while on vacation?

- What is your favorite candy?

- What is your favorite color car?

- What is your favorite family vacation?

- What is your favorite food?

- What is your favorite gas station drink or food?

- What is your favorite license plate design?

- What is your favorite restaurant?

- What is your favorite smell?

- What is your favorite song?

- What is your favorite sound that nature makes?

- What is your favorite thing to bring home from a vacation?

- What is your favorite vacation with friends?

- What is your favorite way to relax?

- Where is the farthest place you ever traveled in a car?

- Where is the farthest place you ever went North, South, East and West?

- Where is your favorite place in the world?

- Who is your favorite singer?

- Who taught you how to drive?

- Who will you miss the most while you are away?

- Who if the first person you will contact when you get to your destination?

- Who brought you on your first vacation?

- Who likes to travel the most in your life?

- Would you rather be hot or cold?

- Would you rather drive above, below, or at the speed limited?

- Would you rather drive on a highway or a back road?

- Would you rather go on a train or a boat?

- Would you rather go to the beach or the woods?